SMALL HABITS

SMALL CHANGES THAT CHANGE EVERYTHING

By

Jude Brown, PhD

Copyright © 2023 Jude Brown, PhD
All rights reserved

TABLE OF CONTENT

Introduction
CHAPTER 1:The Power of Small Changes
CHAPTER 2:Identifying Areas of Your Life to Change
CHAPTER 3:Setting Realistic Goals
CHAPTER 4:Implementing Habits and Routines
CHAPTER 5:The Importance of Mindset
CHAPTER 6:Overcoming Self-Doubt and Procrastination
CHAPTER 7:Making Changes That Stick
CHAPTER 8:The Ripple Effect of Small Changes
CHAPTER 9:Using Failure as a Learning Opportunity
CHAPTER 10:Building a Support System for Success
Conclusion

Introduction

Making small changes that lead to significant improvements in our lives is a process that requires effort and commitment. However, it is important to recognize that these subtle shifts in behavior, habits, and mindset can have a profound impact on our overall well-being, relationships, and personal and professional growth.

The concept of small changes may seem insignificant, but it can be a powerful tool for driving positive change in various aspects of our lives. By focusing on one or two small changes at a time, we can create a domino effect of positive change that influences and improves other areas of our lives.

In this book, we will explore the power of small changes and provide practical strategies for making them a part of our daily lives. We will cover topics such as identifying areas of our lives that could benefit from change, setting realistic goals, implementing new habits and routines, cultivating a positive mindset, overcoming self-doubt and procrastination, and building a support system for success.

By following these strategies and staying consistent and committed, we can make small changes that lead to significant improvements in our lives and ultimately change everything.

CHAPTER 1

The Power of Small Changes

The concept of small changes may seem insignificant, but it can have a significant impact on our lives. These subtle shifts in behavior, habits, and mindset can lead to significant improvements in our overall well-being, relationships, and personal and professional growth.

One practical example of the power of small changes is the concept of "kaizen" in Japanese business culture. Kaizen means continuous improvement and encourages small, incremental changes to processes, systems, and daily routines. This philosophy has been adopted by companies worldwide and has proven to be an effective method for driving efficiency and productivity.

Another example is the "1% rule," which suggests that making small, consistent improvements in a particular area can lead to significant progress over time. For instance, increasing exercise by just 1% each day can lead to a noticeable difference in physical fitness after a few months.

Small changes can also have a positive impact on our mental health. Instead of trying to overhaul our entire lives, making small adjustments to our daily routines and habits can help us feel more in control and reduce stress and anxiety. For instance, taking a few minutes each day to practice mindfulness or setting aside time for self-care can make a big difference in our overall well-being.

In conclusion, the power of small changes should not be underestimated. These subtle shifts in behavior and mindset can lead to significant improvements in various aspects of our lives and can ultimately change everything.

CHAPTER 2

Identifying Areas of Your Life to Change

Before making small changes, it is important to identify the areas of our lives that we want to improve. This may involve evaluating our current habits, routines, and mindset to determine what is and isn't working for us.

One practical way to identify areas of our lives that could benefit from small changes is to reflect on our goals and values. What are the most important things to us? What do we want to achieve or improve? By aligning our daily habits and routines with our values and goals, we can create a sense of purpose and direction in our lives.

Another method is to pay attention to our emotions and physical well-being. Do we often feel stressed, anxious, or overwhelmed? Do we struggle with physical health issues or unhealthy habits? Identifying and addressing these challenges can lead to significant improvements in our overall well-being.

It is also important, to be honest with ourselves about our limitations and challenges. Making small changes can be difficult, and it is important to recognize that we may not be able to change everything at once. By being honest with ourselves and setting realistic goals, we can create a plan that is both achievable and sustainable.

In conclusion, identifying the areas of our lives that could benefit from small changes is an important step in the process of creating positive change. By evaluating our goals, values, emotions, and physical well-being, we can determine what changes will have the most impact on our overall well-being and happiness.

CHAPTER 3

Setting Realistic Goals

Setting goals is an essential step in making small changes that lead to significant improvements in our lives. However, it is important to set goals that are both achievable and realistic.

One practical way to set realistic goals is to use the SMART criteria: Specific, Measurable, Attainable, Relevant, and Time-bound. By setting goals that are specific and measurable, we can track our progress and see how far we have come. Ensuring that our goals are attainable and relevant to our values and priorities helps us stay motivated and focused. Setting a time frame for our goals helps us stay accountable and creates a sense of urgency.

It is also important to start small. Rather than trying to overhaul our entire lives at once, it is more effective to focus on one or two small changes at a time. This allows us to build momentum and develop new habits that can be sustained over the long term.

Another practical tip is to break down our goals into smaller, more manageable tasks. This can help us stay motivated and focused on making progress, even if we are not seeing immediate results.

In conclusion, setting realistic goals is an important step in the process of making small changes that lead to significant improvements in our lives. By using the SMART criteria and starting small, we can create a plan that is both achievable and sustainable.

CHAPTER 4

Implementing Habits and Routines

Habits and routines play a significant role in our daily lives and can either support or hinder our efforts to make small changes. Implementing new habits and routines can be challenging, but with a little planning and effort, it is possible to create lasting change.

One practical way to implement new habits is to make use of trigger points or cues. These are specific events or activities that can serve as a reminder to engage in a new behavior. For instance, if we want to start exercising more, we could set a trigger point by tying our new habit to an existing one, such as going for a walk after dinner each night.

Another useful strategy is to start small and gradually build up. Rather than trying to implement a new habit all at once, we can start with a small, achievable goal and gradually increase the frequency or intensity over time. This helps us build momentum and creates a sense of accomplishment as we make progress.

It is also important to be patient and kind to ourselves as we implement new habits. We may encounter setbacks and challenges, and it is important to recognize that it takes time and effort to develop new habits. By staying consistent and committed, we can create lasting change.

In conclusion, implementing new habits and routines is an important step in the process of making small changes that lead to significant improvements in our lives. By using trigger points, starting small, and being patient and kind to ourselves, we can create lasting change and develop habits that support our goals and values.

CHAPTER 5

The Importance of Mindset

Our mindset plays a significant role in our ability to make small changes that lead to significant improvements in our lives. A positive, growth-oriented mindset can help us overcome challenges and setbacks, while a negative, fixed mindset can hinder our progress and limit our potential.

One practical way to cultivate a growth mindset is to focus on learning and personal development. Rather than viewing challenges as failures, we can see them as opportunities to learn and grow. This can help us stay motivated and resilient when faced with setbacks.

Another useful strategy is to surround ourselves with supportive and positive people. Our social network can have a significant impact on our mindset and behavior, and by surrounding ourselves with individuals who encourage and support us, we can foster a positive and growth-oriented mindset.

It is also important to practice gratitude and focus on the positive aspects of our lives. This helps us cultivate a sense of appreciation and contentment and can help us stay motivated and focused on making small changes that lead to significant improvements.

In conclusion, cultivating a positive and growth-oriented mindset is an important step in the process of making small changes that lead to significant improvements in our lives. By focusing on learning and personal development, surrounding ourselves with supportive people, and practicing gratitude, we can foster a mindset that supports our goals and values.

CHAPTER 6

Overcoming Self-Doubt and Procrastination

Self-doubt and procrastination are common barriers that can hinder our efforts to make small changes that lead to significant improvements in our lives. However, with a little planning and effort, it is possible to overcome these challenges and make progress.

One practical way to overcome self-doubt is to practice self-compassion. Rather than criticizing ourselves for our shortcomings, we can recognize that everyone makes mistakes and that it is a natural part of the learning and growth process. By being kind and understanding with ourselves, we can build confidence and resilience.

Another useful strategy is to seek out supportive and positive people who can provide encouragement and guidance. This can help us stay motivated and focused on making progress, even when we encounter challenges.

To overcome procrastination, it is important to set clear and specific goals and to break them down into smaller, more manageable tasks. This can help us stay focused and motivated and can prevent us from becoming overwhelmed. It is also useful to establish a regular routine and set aside dedicated time for working towards our goals.

In conclusion, overcoming self-doubt and procrastination is an important step in the process of making small changes that lead to significant improvements in our lives. By practicing self-compassion, seeking out supportive people, and setting clear and specific goals, we can stay motivated and focused on making progress.

CHAPTER 7

Making Changes That Stick

Making small changes that lead to significant improvements in our lives is a process that requires effort and commitment. However, it is important to recognize that changes don't happen overnight and that it takes time and effort to develop new habits and routines.

One practical way to ensure that our changes stick is to create a supportive environment. This may involve making adjustments to our physical space, such as organizing our home or office to support our goals or seeking out supportive friends and colleagues who can encourage and motivate us.

Another useful strategy is to build accountability into our plan. This can be as simple as sharing our goals and progress with a trusted friend or mentor or joining a support group or accountability group. Having someone to hold us accountable can help us stay motivated and on track.

It is also important to be patient and kind to ourselves as we make changes. We may encounter setbacks and challenges, and it is important to recognize that it takes time and effort to develop new habits and routines. By staying consistent and committed, we can create lasting change.

In conclusion, making small changes that lead to significant improvements in our lives requires effort and commitment. By creating a supportive environment, building accountability into our plan, and being patient and kind to ourselves, we can create lasting change and develop habits and routines that support our goals and values.

CHAPTER 8

The Ripple Effect of Small Changes

Making small changes that lead to significant improvements in our lives can have a ripple effect, influencing and improving other areas of our lives as well. By focusing on one or two small changes at a time, we can create a domino effect of positive change.

One practical example of the ripple effect of small changes is the concept of "keystone habits," or habits that have a cascading impact on other areas of our lives. For instance, establishing a regular exercise routine can lead to improvements in our physical health, but it can also improve our mental well-being, productivity, and relationships.

Another example is the impact of small changes on our mindset and perspective. By focusing on learning and personal development, we can cultivate a growth-oriented mindset that influences our behavior and decision-making. This can lead to improvements in our relationships, career, and overall well-being.

It is important to recognize that the ripple effect of small changes takes time and that it is a process that unfolds over time. By staying consistent and committed, we can create lasting change and improve various aspects of our lives.

In conclusion, the ripple effect of small changes should not be underestimated. By focusing on one or two small changes at a time and staying consistent and committed, we can create a domino effect of positive change that influences and improves other areas of our lives.

CHAPTER 9

Using Failure as a Learning Opportunity

Making small changes that lead to significant improvements in our lives is a process that involves effort and commitment. However, it is important to recognize that we may encounter setbacks and failures along the way. Rather than viewing these challenges as failures, we can use them as opportunities to learn and grow.

One practical way to use failure as a learning opportunity is to reflect on what went wrong and what we can do differently in the future. By analyzing our mistakes and challenges, we can identify patterns and make adjustments to our approach.

Another useful strategy is to seek out feedback and guidance from others. By talking to trusted friends, mentors, or colleagues, we can gain valuable insights and perspectives on our challenges and how to overcome them.

It is also important to be kind and compassionate with ourselves as we encounter failures and setbacks. Recognizing that everyone makes mistakes and that it is a natural part of the learning and growth process can help us stay motivated and resilient.

In conclusion, using failure as a learning opportunity is an important step in the process of making small changes that lead to significant improvements in our lives. By reflecting on our mistakes and seeking out feedback and guidance, we can learn from our failures and make adjustments to our approach to create lasting change.

CHAPTER 10

Building a Support System for Success

Making small changes that lead to significant improvements in our lives is a process that requires effort and commitment. However, it can be challenging to go it alone, and building a support system can help us stay motivated and on track.

One practical way to build a support system is to seek out mentors or advisors who can provide guidance and encouragement. These individuals can offer valuable insights and perspectives and can help us stay motivated and focused on our goals.

Another useful strategy is to join a support group or accountability group. By connecting with others who are working towards similar goals, we can build a sense of community and camaraderie that can help us stay motivated and focused on making progress.

It is also important to build support and accountability into our daily routines and habits. Sharing our goals and progress with a trusted friend or family member can help us stay accountable and motivated.

In conclusion, building a support system is an important step in the process of making small changes that lead to significant improvements in our lives. By seeking out mentors, joining a support group, and building support and accountability into our daily routines, we can create a network of individuals who can encourage and motivate us as we work towards our goals.

Conclusion

In conclusion, making small changes that lead to significant improvements in our lives is a process that requires effort and commitment. By identifying the areas of our lives that could benefit from change, setting realistic goals, implementing new habits and routines, cultivating a positive mindset, overcoming self-doubt and procrastination, and building a support system, we can create lasting change and improve various aspects of our lives.

To ensure success, it is important to start small and gradually build up, to be patient and kind to ourselves as we encounter setbacks and challenges, and to stay consistent and committed. By focusing on one or two small changes at a time and using failure as a learning opportunity, we can create a domino effect of positive change that influences and improves other areas of our lives.

Overall, the power of small changes should not be underestimated. These subtle shifts in behaviour and mindset can lead to significant improvements in our well-being, relationships, and personal and professional growth. By making small changes that lead to significant improvements in our lives, we can change everything.

www.ingramcontent.com/pod-product-compliance
Lightning Source LLC
Chambersburg PA
CBHW050321220526
45465CB00005B/2082